Step into my Green World:

Awakening
Through Walking Meditation

Libby Leyrer

Balboa Press books may be ordered through booksellers or by contacting:

Balboa Press
A Division of Hay House
1663 Liberty Drive
Bloomington, IN 47403
www.balboapress.com
1 (877) 407-4847

Because of the dynamic nature of the Internet, any web addresses or links contained in this book may have changed since publication and may no longer be valid. The views expressed in this work are solely those of the author and do not necessarily reflect the views of the publisher, and the publisher hereby disclaims any responsibility for them.

Any people depicted in stock imagery provided by Getty Images are models, and such images are being used for illustrative purposes only. Certain stock imagery © Getty Images.

ISBN: 978-1-9822-4703-4 (sc)
ISBN: 978-1-9822-4702-7 (e)

Library of Congress Control Number: 2020908802

Print information available on the last page.

Balboa Press rev. date: 05/20/2020

Step Into My Green World:

Awakening Through Walking Meditation

By Libby Leyrer

Dedicated to my dear friend & fellow explorer
G. Alan Marlatt

Table of Contents

Introduction

*W*hat I couldn't know when I started my morning walks is that they would become my literal path to awakening. It began in early spring 2002 with a decision to replace my wake-up ritual of coffee & "The Today Show" with coffee & a walk in the nearby arboretum. It soon became a walking meditation, a commitment first thing every morning to meet & traverse the world of nature with an open heart. In the autumn of that year I added the component of writing about the experience. The writing reflected my connection to & reverence of nature, its cycles, the interplay between my inner & outer world. At times the form is revealed in fragments; I leave these uncorrected. This spontaneous expression informed my spiritual journey along the path of my daily meditation.

Let me also give you some background, an introduction to me personally. I grew up in the 50s & 60s in a fairly "normal" upper middle class family. I survived two near death experiences before I reached the age of ten. I also started having migraine headaches at age eight, in primary school. Then at twelve I broke my tailbone slipping & crashing on concrete steps. The reason I mention these early details of my childhood is that I came to understand their relevance & connectedness in later years. I learned from one of my shaman-spiritual guides that the migraines & broken tailbone were necessary to enlarge my capability to receive & channel the enormous amount of energy coming into my body. The near death events proved insightful; the second one introduced me to an angel who swept me up from the path of a car that would have run me over. I remember thinking after the event that I must have been put on this earth for a reason. In my early teens I started experimenting with mind expanding & hallucinogenic drugs. I discovered the meaning of life while experiencing "cosmic consciousness" in the middle of the night at a rock festival. I was sixteen. I supplemented middle & high school with hours in the public library studying Eastern philosophy, reading existential novels, & delving into many of life's mysteries. I was initiated into Transcendental Meditation at the age of eighteen. I am a life long explorer.

The fragrance has changed. The fermented leaf-apple scent has been infused with the green freshness of cedar, fir & pine. The crush of the mix, the full breath bringing the Christmas smell directly to the child within. Where are the birds, the squirrels? Today they are hiding, except for the crows, the moving carpet of night: harbinger of winter, the dark dream. I will light a candle. My heart is warm, my eyes clear…still miles & miles.

This morning broke golden & blue; a direct hit on all my senses. As I entered my forest of enchantment there was a mist lifting from the earth's body like steam off a warm body after a bath. Following my path I went under the long lacy fingers of cedar newly decorated with crystal drops. The witchy trees were strewn & lit with the same delicate beads, reflecting the world, waiting, weighting to drop eventually…the motion, however slow, never ends.

A beautiful, moist morning with lively undercurrents. I am able to feed on the quiet stark branches lit from below by the thick leaf mosaic. It is bouncing color & texture into the air, into me. I think about a question, am I happy. Something I discovered along my inner travels is that there is a place not on any map, deep within me. It is all the colors of light & all the colors of joy & peace & love. I make a conscious donation to that place every morning when I talk to my trees & love them, when I take in & appreciate the amazing life I've been given. I am so happy I could burst. I am also sad & the complete range/shades of imaginable emotion. I am yin & yang. I am not separate.

My walk was a head clearer after a night of too much champagne & too little sleep. The birds were happy & lively. Mushrooms have sprung up to become fairy villages on berms of woodland groundcover. I saw a chubby squirrel showing off his physique climbing down a tree. Right now I'm watching a crow navigate the gutters of the house next door, selectively picking out leaves trying to uncover morsels for snacking.

Biting moisture flooding my nose. The fog brings everything closer, like a soft quilt pulling the world into a pile. I'm all alone in my misty place, the sounds are muffled, the taste of the air peculiar. As I walk I think of the Northwest Masters, specifically Mark Tobey & Morris Graves & their use of white paint- the mystic writing. I see it in the banks & drifts of fog, the overlay. They knew this world.

Early walk today, pink breaking the edges of the horizon, a perfect bright half moon in a perfect sky. The quiet beauty stirs & soothes me. My wonderful daughter is here for two weeks. She has blossomed during her five months on the east coast. It is intoxicating for me to spend time with her.

Walking, moving through space, visual barrage, enormous amounts of information, senses grabbing, receiving, exploring. Thinking streams connecting into thoughts of how I find my way in this world, how I interpret & act on my sensory feast. Early on I sought physical risk. I was a tomboy, started ski racing at age ten, continuing to ski straight down the mountain, breathing the exhilaration, pushing speed to the edge. I remember consciously slowing down when my first child was born, knowing that she needed me to be around. To celebrate my freedom from what had become an unworkable marriage, I started skydiving. Twice I brought the kids to watch & they got to see their mom flying, twirling, thrusting & floating down to earth.

Fog has set in. A somber half-dream, sounds & colors stripped of their edge & potency. Time is stretched, the fabric of place has changed; the warp & weft dissolving, then reforming, patterns shifting. I find a pentagram of leaves. The fairy-wiccan have been at work. I move through this & the melody of song fills me & stays with me until I am safely home.

The rain started in the night; my path has small rivers & lakes to show for it. The trees are dressed in their beads once again but it is a quiet celebration, no fanfare. The light is subdued & I emerge from the tunnel seeking a larger, brighter place.

So many scattered thoughts hovered in my brain as I started the trail. As I attended to each & released it, I felt my load lighten. The movement is key for me. I need to physically experience my world, my life. Sometimes at night while

I'm driving alone I crank up the music, open the windows, push the speed to flood my senses. It is at the edges that I feel most alive, engaged...the depths, the heights, the extremes.

There is magic afoot; something in the air. I found myself laughing & dancing along the path...breathing everything in, finding my playful self & literally running with it. As I was leaving the woods I saw the tiniest hummingbird sitting atop a tree. I stopped to watch her & of course tell her how wonderful she is. She stayed for about half a minute then whirred off. I'd seen one in my yard a couple of weeks ago near my deep orange trumpet flower (they like red & orange), but I thought they'd have migrated by now. I've read that hummingbirds migrate thousands of miles; can you imagine? I looked up Hummingbird in my Medicine Card book. She represents JOY.

Walking through fine mist is a little like swimming under water with eyes open. There's a distance between worlds, a degree of pressure. I am a quiet observer this morning, my footfalls blending with the muted chattering of tiny birds & the shifting of the soggy leaf carpet. Finding my center, I am prepared for the day.

The trees are holding on to the night. The sky beyond is separate, lifting white into blue from the mist below. It gave me an idea. I'm going to have a cloak made, reversible; one side day, the other night, with dawn & dusk colors transitioning between.

Building my Faith

I'm thinking about how I need every step of my walk, of my journey. There is something of value in each piece, each glance, thought, movement, connection. I'm building my faith. I see it reflected in the exquisite perfection of nature; the cycle of seasons, each giving way to the next, expressing life, death, rebirth.

The rain felt good. It stayed with me the entire walk, washing my face & letting me be part of the glistening, moist world. Thoughts of death, letting go, vulnerability, growing older, love; the movement, the pace, the change of light, scenery...a treasure.

The spaces are changing, the carpet thickening & the sky opening. I'm feeling primitive, preverbal this morning, connecting with the primordial spirits of the woods. I'm stepping through my tunnel, pulling from the outside in.

It was dark when I crossed the bridge to enter my forest. The lamps threw light on the edges of long puddles along the bridge way. My trees were sleeping. I walked quietly in anticipation. As the light returned, there were a thousand shades of green; a chorus of a thousand voices.

As I walked out the door I saw two boys waiting for their ride to school. The bigger boy was bouncing a basketball, not with much enthusiasm. The smaller boy took off his backpack so he could play, but at that very moment the older boy accessed the situation & created a power struggle/division instead of a connection. He turned away & taunted the littler boy. As I turned the corner I heard the cries from the younger boy. An age-old dynamic, demonstrating how evolution sometimes moves very slowly.

Winter 2002/Solstice Morning

Solstice morning, feeling the awakening, a subtle sound accompanies the curtain opening. The first day of winter, activity going underground, the earth sleeps. My external nature is drawn in to the internal. I feel calm.

Cold & clear, the quiet is in place; we are all here in ceremony. I am part of the Circle.

Cold, damp, slightly acrid edge to the mist, I warm up as I enter the heart of my woods. I am finding new depths, carving new designs in the caverns within myself. Now they are runes, hieroglyphs. I cannot read them yet.

Moving through textures, light playing on surfaces, tricking the eye; trompe l'oeil, finding a multitude of colors of berries; fire red, purple, golden, orange, white, pale cranberry to deep grape. Soft pussy willow textures caressing, seducing; harsh, barren textures forging a contrast with the playful blossoms that reveal the promise of beauty & life.

My forest was full of sound this morning. The air was almost warm & there was a mysterious quality to the light, a slight cast of violet. The trees were dancing, making the wind visible & I felt a rush as the wind sound amplified & tunneled into me. It pulled the rain off the leaves to make water music. Sensory bliss. I left feeling filled to the brim.

Nature had her way with my green world; there was no place on my path that remained unchanged. Boughs & limbs of fir & cedar were everywhere. Shards of bark, crushed sticks, roots, leaves, even the white petals from winter camellia blossoms decorated this new place. Creation birthed from destruction.

Entering my forest I felt a relaxed & cheerful tone. The birds were busy & happy, the sun invigorating the open spaces. The sky had patches of blue. I thought of my father. My brother & I grew up learning that the weather would clear up if there was enough blue in the sky to make a Dutchman's britches. The autumn months were

Septober, Octember & Nowonder. His favorite color was skyblue-pink. My father would devour literature & collect dirty limericks. He was the best kind of father because he would really play with us; he never lost the child within. The last time I saw my father was three days before he died; I was hand-feeding him chocolate truffles & he was radiantly blissful.

Near the end of my walk I reached the rhododendron bush in full rosy-pink bloom & I noticed a slight movement. My hummingbird! I stood really still & she gathered nectar from several blossoms, perched for a moment on a branch, went back to feeding. She showed me her green & blue belly & her golden back & then she flew away.

The earth is drinking, all her surfaces pulling the moisture in, the sounds soft & musical. The creeks now move & sparkle & sing. The trees stand nourished & strong.

The woods had a quiet texture. The trees whispered to me in an ancient language, beckoning the Mysteries, opening a gateway.

Late walk, I enjoyed being bundled up against the rain, feeling warm & protected. The earth continues to drink. The trees reveal their dark, shiny, naked skins, limbs contorting & corresponding to each of their neighbors: jungle dancers. I'm feasting on leftover Chinese noodles; my body craving their greasy flavorful comfort.

Wore my long coat & snow boots today. I wanted to be able to splash through the puddles. When I reached the forest I suddenly felt very small. My boots had become the slicker boots of my childhood & everything around me gained an added dimension. About half way through, it started pouring & I opened my coat to get soaked to the skin. I turned my face to the sky; its bones & contours became terrain for rivers. When I emerged, the rain had stopped & I found quiet puddles. Once again the world has changed by my stepping into it.

The new light was welcome after the dark mornings. There was a buoyancy to the energy; the critters felt it. I watched a parade of squirrels scallop across my path. The bushes were full of the rustles of tiny birds. The streams & ponds were fat & happy.

Predawn/New Ground, New Pain

My monthly blood is bringing me to my underground river where every tear is stored, where I must go to celebrate my inner depths. It is lonely & dark; the water is cold. There are new places inside me. I find the quiet runes & hieroglyphs. I find my carving tool. The blade is sharp, the cuts deep…new ground, new pain. I am walking in faith.

The rain brings me farther along my river. The moody places along my path speak to the waters. I am again alone. I yearn to hear your voice.

The sky is a pristine Nordic blue with feathery clouds giving it dimension. The air is clean, tasting of cool golden light. The birds are everywhere. Deep in the woods I saw a new one, the size of a robin but very fancy; orange & deep gray, black & a bit of white. His beak is longer than a robin's & there's a sleekness about him. Below the shelter there was a field of crows, their black figures dramatically offset by the burnt-orange leaves they grazed in. The lookout crow in a tree above made notice of me & I assured him I meant no harm. He seemed to understand & was silent.

There was a curtain of mist around my green world. I was entering a secret place. The bird song was so sweet & so pure, the sounds seemed amplified, filling me up. I am so blessed, this moment, my peaceful heart.

Artic blue-white sky, frosted landscape, I've retreated into my inner shelter. My eyes burn, my breath vapors, the only witness my long shadow.

I enter my place of worship, the towering evergreens in their vestments, smaller acolytes standing by. The choir has no need of hymnals. I fulfill a moving sacrament, whispering my prayers to the waiting trees.

The cold air seemed to bring my senses into sharp focus. The witch hazel blossoms blasted their scent from afar, as the great blue heron shook the earth with his prehistoric squawk. The ground was slippery with a hard crust, taking away any carefree stepping. Winter has spoken; its serious gray spread into the inside, taken root, slumber dancing slowly into death.

The earth gradually awakened, its frosted coating making the colors in the light dance. Walking into the forest tunnels became a study in subtleties & low light. Returning to the open spaces I watched the colors catch fire.

First you walk, then you run & sometimes you just stand still. I think I need to stand still for a moment, survey my life, my surroundings; allow what's here to come in, to integrate, to enrich.

My walk was many things today; a breathing meditation, an invocation of thoughts & desires, the possibility of an exorcism. The space was calm & welcoming. I felt safe. I walk, I think, I learn, I try to understand, I grapple.

Such a moist, succulent place my green world; its round beauty reflecting the colors of the sky, the colors of beyond, the limitless.

As I walked briskly through my green world I felt I was following a current, a mutual caress. The dramatic moss-covered maples commanded my admiration, their branches stretching into the mystery of the skies. I found new dark places; shapes were revealed by the brothers & sisters. Together we found the unspoken meeting place.

There was an exquisitely subtle mist on the edges of my green place. The muted colors drifted into me & nourished me. I found the quiet center & brought it home.

There is a conspiracy; the moon, my inner tides, the movie I went to see last night. I'm so full, electrified. My passage through the woods this morning served as a filter for the many thoughts & ideas charging through my brain. I needed the grounding. There is so much in my life to orchestrate; I know I've chosen this life. It fits me like a glove.

Beams of sunlight penetrated the mist, searing the expanse of crystalized landscape. I walked into the dark center, finding my microcosm, my finite place, the world reflected in each drop of water captured on the tiny fingers splayed out from lacy green hands.

Quiet appreciation for my green world; moment by moment feeling the exchange of energy, of understanding & then the merging.

Transformation: Whispering Ancient Friends, My Ghost Tree

More grounding after active night; moving, soothing, breathing, absorbing, pulling, being. There are places on my path that guide me, instruct my inner being. I am transformed by the rocks, the whispering ancient friends, my ghost tree.

The sounds were juicy, indelicate & joyful in my greedy wet world. As I became a river surging along my path, it occurred to me that it might be time to start writing about what came before: my movies. So much has been thrust into consciousness of late, the stirring of muddy, murky depths. Perhaps it is time to breathe life into Libby's truly amazing misadventures.

My walk was very early today out of necessity. I entered my forest in darkness. As I moved along the path, it felt a different journey. The wind cooled my flushed face, the excitement of my stretched senses trying to fill the space. The fatter than half moon was encircled in pink. I'm just thinking about how I like having the forest to myself, when a gang of crows reminds me with their cries that it is their place too. They swiftly cross the pink clouds beneath the moon. As I'm passing through the last of my woods, there is the slightest suggestion of color, just a hint of what is to be, but is not yet.

Today I felt as if I were walking in a dream. I've been doing so much of my work in the middle of the night, when the veils are thinned & the fabric of time & memory pulses recognition. The day has become my dreamtime.

A slice of springtime. The cherry tree on the way to the Winter garden has popped its first blossoms. An early celebration!

Storm & rain in the night. As I enter my green place the enormous, fluffy clouds are being swept by the tops of the swaying trees. The wind is everywhere. I take a breath. There is new skin on the earth. I follow my path through more wonderful turbulence, then out to the clearing where the sky reappears blue &

bright, the sweetest trilling coming from the happy birds. I pass my hummingbird tree. She looks the Prom Queen the morning after; dress torn, lipstick smudged, still pretty but in a different, more knowing way. We have both been taken by the wind.

Today I felt each step, the gravitational pull taking advantage of my sleep-deprived body. I've started examining why I seem resistant to writing about my past. There is so much richness in what is now. There are no doubt other dreads...I must just begin & see what happens.

Wonderful brisk walk, finding my rhythm, letting everything come in, breath to breath, step to step. I feel a bit like I've been gently brushed, my tangles taken out.

My walk in my glistening dark world today was a song. I sang my love to the trees; I chanted all along the way, touching the branches, the leaves, fronds, blossoms, spires, bracts. I chanted my emptiness into fullness & my fullness into emptiness. I was a vessel of song.

Quiet walk, just passing through; flat light, puddles muddy. Near midway I walked through the mist into my tunnel where the mild temperatures are coaxing the leaf buds to open. A dangerous folly in midwinter, but the new life is uplifting & more precious because of the uncertainty.

With the wind, my partner in the promise of change & cleansing of the mind, I dream my walk suspended in an airy channel. I find my way back in time to witness an auspicious Chinese tableau: a Great Blue Heron standing next to a still pond. Serenity, Strength, Beauty, Reflection.

I awoke with the energy of a thousand kings. The light fed me as I moved into my place of reverence. The streams were singing, the sunlight, textures & colors reflecting nature's perfection. Another auspicious moment as I entered the shelter: two lovers kissing. I returned home in sweet fullness.

The journey brought me into that other place where light shifts color & sounds become texture. The congregation of crows set stage in & around the perfect white birch. It was a piece of a dream, a fragment out of time; their raucous voices drawing me to them as if through a tunnel. They were sent by big brother Raven who foretold it in my cards yesterday. There is magic afoot, in the time of the dark moon, in Aquarius' shadow, a shift. It has taken residence in my emptiness.

Long strides took me quickly over the contours of my familiar place. Feeling the implicit agreement, I took license to explore. There is a new aliveness, a swelling, opening, bursting. It has moved into me & I am grateful for this gift.

Inward journey, quiet, rhythmic. Still gathering & feeling the peace.

My heart started racing when I saw the fog. I wanted to jump into another dimension. My green world was transformed. The fog both accentuated & masked at its whim. The majestic cedars & firs circled, creating a moving perspective; wisps of fog wrapping & nestling, sheets & pillows of fog jostling & hiding the light & the edges of the world.

The frost had started to soften as I left the house. There was a beautiful crystal painting on a car window. The fog had reentered my forest, but was being slowly chased away by the sunlight. I felt the cold like a weight inside me. I carry it still.

I'm thinking about why I'm drawn to the fog & often characterize it in terms relating to sleep. I realize right now I'm quite vulnerable to a dark voice within me. Today the fog was laced with blue & gold & pink glimmers, drifting high up to distort the tops of the trees. Its seduction was of a different sort; not the opium dream, more the dance of Shiva.

Cold morning, many thoughts: contentment, beauty, gratitude.

I am grateful for my green place, so much is revealed to me as I move through. Today I felt the pure pleasure of fluid movement; running, feeling the strength of my legs, the pumping of blood into my heart, the breath moving in & out of my lungs, the perfect miracle of my body.

Moving into my forest I was filled with the disturbance & sadness of the night before, the unrest. The tenuousness of faith, working with so little information, taking cues from the air & the silence.

Part of my walking meditation gave me thoughts of my mother. She was a wonderful celebration yesterday. In her home, amidst loved ones she shined. Her wit & charm effused from her effortlessly. Our appreciation & laughter fed & encouraged her. It gives me such pleasure to see her in her element, & so happy.

True enchantment: a frozen world bursting with the energy of new life, new openings. Renewing my faith, putting the treachery of my dreams behind me, at least for now.

I am in transition. My tears soften the inner earth for excavation. I polish my tools & taste the anticipation of pain. As I go back I go forward. The blood trail, I do see it from this distance. The blood which took my innocence. The blood when I cut his initials in my arm with a razor blade. The possession of pain, of the marking, the claiming.

Thick blanket of fog, quiet place. I found my receptive-feminine, gathering & pulling into myself, the place, the journey, the experience. I will sit with this & just breathe.

Nature cranked it up a notch. In keeping with my desire to remain in receptive-feminine mode, I inhaled the magnified beauty of my green world.

Just paying attention allowed me to come out of myself. I'm at a place where my questions are taking me into uncharted territory. Revisiting beneath memory, beyond comfort, blind undaunted faith.

I am being stirred by everything that touches me. My path brought me to deep contractions of sadness, cold tears leading to more mystery. I feel everything that enters me, but it doesn't find its place; it just crowds in & suffocates my senses. It is a bombardment; I am laid waste.

I experienced a cleansing, a reawakening, another chance to see & receive the quiet essence.

The bird song wove me into the waking dream. Inside I found the earth newly imbedded by the strong night rain. The sunlight cast its colors onto the painterly sky as the clouds told their story.

As I entered the fragile glass orb that was my world today, I traveled through my own tears. They were few, but brought me to a new precision & depth, without the familiar sadness. The language of the skies beyond the trees stirred a voice within me. I carry the ages; my bones connect with the ancient songs before time.

Monkeys Swans & Lions

My plate has been filled of late with a diverse feast. Inspiration in the form of whimsical ink monkeys, swans & lions. In another segment, egg temperas, gouaches, washes & blocks of color applied through blood memory to continue the story of a people. We are all telling our story, the rewards & costs are varied, the methods as well.

Passing "the dancers", a tree configuration early in my walk, I'm thinking what a wonderful sculpture it is. The graceful relationship of the trunks creates the two dancers, her mossy skirt flowing, his two legs retaining the stopped movement of the dance.

Today I was a warm beam passing through on my path. The wind teased, guided & reminded me. The gulls described the energy of the sky. The trees have boldly opened, crossed the point of no return. I feel like a co-conspirator. Choose life, choose beauty, snatch death from the shriveled hand of Skeleton Woman. This is a day of my fullness, my completion; the world is inside me, I am the surrender.

By the end of my walk I am full of wellbeing. I've gathered the murmurs & whispers of the wood sprites. I feel the hum of new life underfoot. Tufts & blades of spring greens & yellows are opening new pathways for my spirit.

As I play hide & seek with the sunlight in my green world, streams of birdsong move into me & I feel the life pulse through my feet.

Bright blue, cold sun. The hardened earth has a layer of sparkle dust. Ice has formed on the puddles. Inside my green place I find the spring celebration of yesterday has bowed forlornly into itself. Leaves once open & jubilant are now scrolling & tent like, shrinking against their aggressor. I can only whisper to them what they already know.

Clear cold light. Sleeping Beauty coverlet lay over the frozen world. The towering evergreens impervious to the new winter stand guard in their timeless reign. Fragile blossoms express translucent beauty as they transition slowly into death after just a moment's glory. It is a world rich in the promise of passage & transcendence.

Here I sit the darkness surrounding me, the stretch of day behind me, my morning walk a distant memory. Somehow though the writing springs from it, the movement not complete without the telling. I will go back in time to retrieve an aspect. I remember thinking about how the physical act of looking up into the sky connected me to my childlike wonder. The physical bowing under a limb of my ghost tree brought me to the reverence of nature. Engaging all my senses brings me untold treasures; they find a place to germinate within me.

Breaking through the surface, again a shift. The sheets of ice on the small pond have melted. The bounty of hellebores no longer genuflect. We are all looking skyward once again as children at the feet of god.

Again changed, washed, replenished. Succulent green places found through secret memory, uncovered by the wanting, a dreamwalk,

Wonderful cool clear morning. Sunlight flooding fields of grass, articulating each glistening blade.

An effortless walk, the light bringing about such ease to my journey; my mind floating, at one with my body.

Gentle curtain of rain drifting in & out, creating pockets of enchantment. Nature's grace & surprise.

Diaphanous moving into earthy, rich, shifts of fancy, circular in nature, ever moving....holding on, letting go, letting grow.

Today I expanded throughout my green world. I looked down every path. I let myself wander & wonder. I thought about my strength, my fluidity, my focus, my ability to embrace all. I touched my trees, I professed my love. I gave myself to this place.

I saw an eagle in flight as I entered my forest. There was a sense of precognition, a stillness & an eerie violet cast to the light. As I reached a narrow pathway the wind sent a giant shiver through my green world. As I left, part of me remained.

Entering a Cartoon

eaving the house the wind hit my face. The gulls were the only birds in the sky; all the others had gone home. I heard the whistle of a loose fan belt. I had suddenly entered a cartoon.

There was a cool moist invitation to my green place. The turbulence of the past days was evident in the scattered pieces of bark & moss. The camellias added their white & pink & almost-fuschia to the color story. The quiet aftermath fed me while my eyes remained the gatherers of that which will be revealed in another way, in another place & time.

It felt good to move after a restless night. I pounced on my green terrain, eager to feel her open arms. I found my rhythm, received her grace, then went inside myself to face my torment. It took awhile but the tears came, the release moved me to run & I came out the other side. I can feel the unwept tears, the further release is waiting. I must find my way there, but now is not the time.

First part of my walk I was all in my head. Then when I realized what was going on I moved into a physical embrace of my green world. I let it fill me up & energize me. I started to breathe again.

The world was clean & sweet with just a whisper of breeze bringing cool mist onto my skin. Moving through I felt the familiar passage, the entrance into my own dimension.

Enveloped in my reverie, I make my trek beyond the music of the rain.

Today I was the storm blowing through my green world. The serene sky witnessed my white-hot fury & my pulsing wails. My physical vessel could not contain what was emanating from the underground otherworld of my unconscious. The shadows masking the clear sight, the layers of hushed voices & stifled cries. I must find my way back, over broken glass disguised as a river of flowers. Follow the blood trail. I am that child.

There is a churning. I find that the more my heart opens to my mother, the more early stuff starts emerging. It's like a circular dance through funhouse mirrors. My mother becoming my child becoming my mother. There is always the sting of her criticism, my vulnerability, how I try to be perfect so I don't have to feel like that girl, to have to disappear. How I learned to not judge, to free myself, to accept. Why can I approach the world in my non-judgment, but not include myself?

Walking through my green place today was an active prayer. The gift of the moss-covered trees contrasted the brilliant pinks & stark sky-grays. The roundness-flatness, dullness-glossiness of the colors created tension, bringing life & activity to the eye.

Brand new day drenched & sparkling. Every step was accompanied by birdsong, a fluidity of orchestration, the sound coming from every direction. In the Winter garden I ducked into the back trails & found the offering I was looking for. I lay down in the bed of fallen white & pink camellia blossoms, closed my eyes & let my other senses take over.

Serene feast, blissed out birds bringing/singing in the new morning. The scattered windfall decorated my meditation, weaving the cool moist flesh of magnolia & camellia blossoms into my musings.

Spring 2003/Quiet Retrieval

Quiet retrieval; Spring emerging, uncovering, rejoicing.

Gentle morning, lively birds, brilliant sunlight. Gaining entrance to my inner world, the tunnel brought me to filtered green coolness & on to the jungle dancers with flowers in their hair the size of cocktail hats. I dance through to the more solemn offerings. The stones in the pathway remind me of the currents & winds affecting my course. I'm a strong sailor, ready to hoist the sail or turn about as life dictates. Right now I'm drifting on calm seas finding peace & contentment.

Everything was the color of the rain, a soggy gray which shrouded my green world. Then as I crossed the little creek where the bright yellow skunk cabbage & newly green fronds of the fiddlehead ferns were springing forth, the full palette returned. I'm stirred by the unknown source, a gift from the deep.

I felt lionine in my movements this morning. I covered my territory with focused attention, aware of the pleasure I derived from the movement itself.

Embarked on my journey in a downpour. The rain intermittently let up, seeming to time dramatic thrusts in just the right parts of my forest. As I came into the open I saw pockets of robin's egg blue nestled in faraway fluffy clouds.

Today I felt invisible & walked through silent forests. The wind reminded me of the ways of the world, the movement through change. I found myself again as I placed a blossom on the altar.

What a beautiful tender morning, all the puddles filled to the brim from last night's rain. The quiet beauty of the spring trees opening their new life for us to celebrate. My emotions change as I travel my path, the long dark sadness moves into acceptance & more sadness-grief.

Pulling peace into myself every step & breath. Passing gentle friends marking the movement of my heart.

Breathtaking beauty, the weeping cherry trees in perfect harmony with the rolling grass, soothing to the eye & uplifting to the spirit. As I spoke my love to the trees I moved it out of my body through my tears.

Quiet entry to my green place. I walk by a grieving bird silently standing on the freshly cut stump of what once was his cedar tree. Nearby lay the stripped logs, lifeless & heavy, effusing the air with sadness. I am the receptive. I will make a place for all of this to make sense. It is the carving that I have begun again in my underground caverns. As I continue much feels unchanged until I nearly reach my jungle dancers. The cherry has released thousands of its tiny pink petals & I walk with delight on this new carpet. As I near the end of my path I feel a seed being planted within me & just as this ripple occurs, the sunlight finds me. I will nurture this mystery & watch it grow.

Not far into the forest I shed another layer through tears. The beauty stirs me to the bubbling over & I'm at the mercy of my unconscious. I make offerings at Nature's altars, touching the surface with my surface, longing for the merging. It came later with the delicate perfection of my chosen blossom. As I was leaving my forest I took a detour to feast on the myriad of cherry trees parading along another path. The subtle color & variety of shapes created balance & movement & utter delight.

There is a progression in the scope & intensity of form & color. I'm enraptured by pairings of lighter than air pinks with dull greens, magenta, translucent apricot with just a flush of rose. The buoyancy & solemnity of shapes, the river of blossoms, cascading & filling me to the brim. Again I find myself in the center of a universe of my own.

The light skittering beneath the trees, in the distance, a piece, a thin horizontal gift which I take with me. There were other gifts; the trillium in bloom, the woodland precious three-petaled perfection. And finding the wonder of this day's new offerings...the gift of WONDER.

Drawn into my green world I was opened once again by the extravagance of its beauty. The wind gently brushed the top of the mighty Arbutus leading me to the sparkling skies. There is a new scent as I walk past the woodland stream & onto the Magnolia petals strewn in abundance, creating the fleshy glow of their own passage. We journey together.

Clear sparkling puddles, washed skies, delicious breaths feeding me the glory of the day. Another shift, receiving blessings, at peace in this skin, belonging to the world.

The wind swept me through my world; finding the edges of me, etching & scraping. I am swallowed by the pain & trust it will take what it needs from me & me from it.

Set out as the frost glistened on the rooftops. Had a series of releases as my sadness intertwined with the misty splendor all around me. As room was made for me to pull in the fullness of the sounds & sights, I felt the healing salve flow & penetrate.

As I was leaving, aware of sadness remaining, I realized the significance of today. My divorce was final exactly seven years ago. Last night in my spring cleaning I'd uncovered the original art for our wedding invitation. No coincidences.

The wind's icy fingers pierced my body as I approached my path, but soon retreated. I received the peaceful passage of my quiet green world but felt my inner currents swirling & encompassing my emotional unrest. There are hopeful glimpses from time to time, but the clearest picture is one of self-exile.

I gradually emptied myself as I traveled my path. I felt the ebb & flow of Nature; the invitation into her process. I looked at the traps I'd set for myself, the ways I'd bent the truth to fit my comfort or image. I am at the beginning of yet another journey, skin shed, eyes wide.

I'm breaking through some old & weathered walls. There is of course incredible resistance. The knowledge that I must look at myself with new eyes, question what I have convinced myself I believe about myself & everything else, is daunting. It is each moment's quest, one unto the next.

Bearing Witness to Life/Death/Life: Finding Divinity

Gentle rain, dancing trees telling an age-old story. I spin through: a flicker. Why do I invite the world through my skin, to wrestle with the tender threads, to pounce into the mystery? I must want to take it on; to ingest it, to transform it through personal alchemy. The fevered energy of passionate love, the transcendent energy of divine love, the power of beauty-seeking bearing witness to the life/death/life in each moment's promise. In this flicker I find my divinity.

Breathing in the patience of the trees, donning the mantle of serenity, I make my way through my green world. If only the mantle were to fit snugly, not slip off & leave me once again bereft.

It is as if the night weavers were at work on the hill above the stream. The fabric of color, light & texture replaced a fallow hillside: a breathtaking vision.

My journey today was a seduction. My green world pulled me in first with the perfume of the cherry blossoms. The scent combined with a delicious tease of warm breeze, then the immersion of open blossoms coloring every moment, every step. As I moved deeper into my world she pulled me closer. I stole some dew to taste as the sunlight captured the glossy essence of the drops nestled on the leaves.

Clear, full newly awakened world
Speaks to me
Enraptures me
It is just enough
I am just enough

As she breathed me in, I felt swept & open & ready to accept the nothingness. I am complete for a moment. Then in the moving, the change of light, the turning of a corner, there enters a thought, a pulse, a rush. I fall into my intensity & am jettisoned from blissful appreciation to deep grief. Somehow it becomes the same: I am on the outside.

My green world totally turned me on today. She was scrubbed clean; the smell of stirred earth filled my lungs. The intricacy & sweetness of the birdsong filled me as well. My whole body was tingling as I found her visual surprises strung throughout my journey. I am still vibrating in communion & completion.

Quiet within & without. The inner workings of my green world are reflected in Life's expression.

The cycle is offering the wisdom of its turning, its ever changing gifts & tariffs. I feel my breath & hear my footfalls & know that I am part of it all.

My drenched green world has a new surface. The leaves, petals & buds wore a finery of tiny drops which glistened & magnified the light. As I entered my tunnel the rain made an instrument of the canopy leaves & I became the percussion walking within the body of the music.

The shifts & contrasts of the early light brought a lively dimension to my green place. The tonic of the movement allowed me to flow. By the end of my walk I found my quiet receptive center.

Opened to the quiet, I moved to the rhythm of beauty. My forest provided sanctuary as well as inspiration.

My eyes were drawn to the distance; the journey became a stretching. The colors blended, soft focus. The moving crows predominated as I threaded through my ever-changing green place. I feel another shift in my inner world, an invitation to explore the caverns.

There was rain in the night. Stepping outside I encountered an enchanted world. The sparkle of the drenched coating on the leaves, flowers & grass merged with the clear fragrant air. Further into my green place I heard the sound of the earth drinking. The evergreens were pushing out new growth the pale green buds giving the trees a more decorative appearance. The intricate melody & rhythm of the birdsong completed my sensory feast.

Walking through my emptiness, feeling it totally surround & inhabit me, I see/feel/recognize a yearning. I want to give myself to this essence, to this void. I am the river that runs through this place, my edges find the sweet earth & are stirred by the open sky. The trees & birds & flowers speak to my center; we fill the world with dreams.

I Listened with my Whole Body

I listened with my whole body. I heard the shout of the orange azalea, the elegant voice of the Japanese cherry. I heard the shifting clouds making way for the pastoral pieces of memory; the blue that reaches back to carefree summer barefoot pleasures. I heard my own breath as I climbed above the pond where the bullfrog sang his love. I heard the rush of my blood as the river of song flowed over me carrying me to the place of quiet reverence.

Somber, quiet fullness, subterranean teachings. My ovaries sang their seed into the web, awakened by the tears that connect my love to the infinite.

I feasted on the delicacies of my green world, the tiny bracts on the maple leaf buds, the fairyland flowers nestled amid the woodland greenery, the fancy bird's long-noted song.

The tunnel of new spring green became a passageway into another realm.

The muted tones filtering through the accompanying vibrant colors became a lively contrast, ever changing. My hillside tapestry is increasing in detail, its subtle design evolving. In my asking for peace & acceptance, I've experienced a breakthrough. My heart is light, a harness released.

I found comfort in the raindrops caressing my cheeks & eyelashes. I felt the current of the earth running through me as I covered my terrain.

There was a vaporous wrap throughout my green world this morning. It moved the blue & gold & white, enmeshing them into the sweetness of my passage. I felt an effortless exchange, a meeting of exquisite tenderness.

Cool breeze, gray skies, the voice of a bullfrog; uplifting, making me smile. Then for the next half-minute a John Cage/Philip Glass piece performed by the restless birds, then a shift into melody. Later on the path a dog reminding me of our family dog, greeted me as if to impart a message. A gift from earlier days; plunging into the matrix once again.

Early in my walk something jogged a memory of another walk. I saw a peregrine falcon in the same area of my woods where I'd witnessed one of nature's dramas early last fall. Here's the unfolding… Just before the bridge into my green world I noticed some feathers. Upon brief scrutiny I understood by the arrangement that they were evidence of a capture. It wasn't until later that I realized this was a foreshadowing. As I continued down my path, around past "the dancers" & into a secluded glade, I happened to look to my right just as a peregrine streaked from a tall evergreen to pounce on his prey. Like a shot from a rifle, so potent in focus, speed, accuracy; fluid in the beauty of death serving life.

I find myself within this majestic chamber listening to my quiet heart; I am a humble journeyer.

Long strides, gentle breeze, the smell of fresh mown grass, all tying deep engagement of the senses to memory & emotion.

I walk, I gather, I breathe, I share. I find my stillness as I travel through this my church of song & branch & sky & stream. I pass through the ages, beyond reach, beyond time.

May Day/Return of my Stellar Jay

As I wandered my path, thoughts came to me, then drifted off. My center drank in the essence of place, of pure beauty, energy & peace. My Stellar Jay has returned; she showed herself to me in the same part of the woods that I'd last seen her several months ago. It is May Day when as a little girl I used to make woven paper baskets, fill them with fresh flowers, put them secretly on my neighbors' porches, ring the bell & run! I still find I am distributing flowers whenever I have them. It is something that I enjoy doing.

I left the house & entered into the distinctly marine air anchoring my world. I found my path to be fluid & welcoming; my thoughts moving with the terrain, bringing quiet recognition & acceptance.

The chill from the night still wrapped my green world. Crossing the bridge the wind joined me, the electric-silver sky sluiced with new spring yellow pulsing penetration. I was swallowed once again & meandered within the belly, gleaning dark messages.

Quiet slow walk along my path, feeling a bit separate, detached. Continuing in a sort of parallel experience, I bumped up against some awkward pieces of myself. As my tears helped me unearth these shards, I found them foreign, unrecognizable. With a degree of lightness, my senses kicked in & there appeared the most perfect fragrant flower the color of honey mixed with butter, smelling of spice & an exhalation of a lover's breath reaching the other's parted lips.

Soon on my path I was overcome with the feeling of tremendous bounty. As I continued, my being swelled to bursting. As I released & breathed my weeping into the air around me, I felt renewed & opened. This took quite a while. It seemed like I was resisting the feeling of wellbeing, the gifts from my world. Again I struggle, I timeshift, the young girl attempting to order the chaos.

Complete surrender to joy

Senses fed
Walking lightly on dew sprinkled grass
Sun streaked path
Gleaming haunted fir trees echo back
To green glass Chartres windows
I drift into the quiet reverie of my inside secret garden

Glorious morning, the light revealing subtle tones, delicious blushes edging the palest apricot. A morning of movement & gathering, reflection. Ob-La-Di Ob-La-Da running through my head. The combination of sleep deprivation & giving in to the waking dream has allowed me to enter my solitude.

On my walk this morning my mantra was Love. I melted into the landscape, my tender parts abutting the stalwart & majestic cedars, the mystical shadow circles just beyond the mist. I feel a fierce connection with this place. It has claimed me.

In quiet reverence I step gently into the melodious current, taking in the wonder & leaving the weight of the physical world behind.

I brought the essence of my green place into my heart, the feelings of peace, beauty, strength, comfort, serenity, inspiration, healing. I invited my green world to come with me on my journey to France. I feel her inside me & will breathe her essence when I want to tap into her treasures & light.

Early Summer 2003/Return from France

First walk since my return from France last night. The re-entry was interesting. My green world feels different, as do I. There is a dryness, a moving into another season, a fullness. I've missed the tiny incremental changes which led to this expanded version of my green place. I feel a bit between two worlds. I haven't quite landed.

Elegant, early morning, golden beams finding passage into my hungry senses. I'm floating through the web of song, the happy flow, loud & fine, I'm back in my green world feet touching the earth. Diving deep I find the center once again, dark with my mystery, the same familiar unknown place where I drop into myself; tumbling, stretching, howling, contracting, another birth. I don't belong here. Je suis toute seule. I am all alone.

The birds heralded the morning. It felt as though I were being presented to the royal court; splendor & beauty abounded. The early sky was shifting warm pale blues into finely sketched clouds: my enchanted world below clear & strong.

It took me awhile today to see the sky. My eye was closer in, the circle drawn. Gradually I allowed my world to enter, to touch me & expand me. I have been walking my inner caverns, the dark pathways glimmering here & there with clues, momentary flashes feeding my faith.

Quiet containment. I feel the building of the weight of my emotions, the feeling a cloud must have before the weight becomes unbearable & rain falls.

Reveling in my sun drenched green world, life bursting in every direction, I took in her gifts with eager breaths. After writing in the night, I opened an entryway to healing & understanding. My steps were lighter, my gaze extended; I'd crashed the gates of my self-made prison.

My inner world is seeking transit to the resounding beauty & life energy of my green world. Through breathing & contemplation the connection is made. I've lived in turbulence these past few days; out of my body, no center.

The sensual interplay of the golden light caressing the lush green textures feeds my spirit. My walk is a gathering & a journey. I have returned to my body.

I entered my enchanted place drawn by bold swaths of light. I have such a physical/sensual relationship with this place; an electrical connection, emotional & spiritual as well. As I breathed in the moist earthy essence, I found bliss. Mushrooms, spicy azaleas, the scent of clove, all there surrounding me, drifting in & out of my range, a lovely palette.

Entering my thirsty sparkling world, I enjoyed watching her drink. Striding through sprinklers, instant summer rush-freedom-childhood glee, I found myself running, loping, gliding, time shifting, spinning….

Early morning, cool fragrant air, bare arms, open senses, the steady rhythm of my steps brought my world inside. My openness came from going inside myself & being still. My inner voice was quiet, inviting completion. I am filled with love, textures, light, colors & birdsong.

Some days feel like beginnings. My faith & strength are reflected in my majestic green world today.

Autumn 2003/Creative Intention

I feel an intense belief in my ability to create my dreams, articulate my vision. I have blind spots, weaknesses; I will need help, but that is part of building a community, an artistic center, a family of creative intention.

Reverence, quiet blessings, peaceful heart, fullness of place, completion. There is everything here in my green world; life, death, every incremental transition in between. Reflection of spirit, beauty, song, the energy of the elements, the secret to the inner workings, to divinity, the code that connects the shadow to the light. When I am here, you are with me, you are me.

I was fully open to my green world. The misty curtain of rain mixed with my tears as I saw the ancient feet of god in the roots of a tree. The movement of my journey brought other gifts into my tender heart.

Back in my forest I felt at first she wanted to exact penance for my absence. She pulled the tears from me, leaving me bereft. As I found my way again, she accepted my offerings, my placements, the symbols marking acknowledgement of the elements, the sharing of beauty, the ritual of giving oneself to find meaning.

My green world was full, overflowing, water reflected everywhere. The trees & plants were swollen with it, bowed down under its burden. They sung sweetly, wetly. The smell & sounds of the earth & streams penetrated me. I became a vessel taking my turn flowing through this lush place, gathering the world into me through my skin.

Wet shiny, entering my new round world, small details. I found my breath, its rhythm helping me to move through- the path, my experience, my emotions.

Quiet inner journey, messages from the plaintive trees.

Birds filled my green world with music today. The wind mixed the rustling of leaves into the song. My path took me where I needed to go: an acceptance, a healing.

Cool & still, the grey pervades as I make my way on light feet, passing the remnants of other dreams, frozen time. I'm trying to turn the page, see what's on the other side. I find a piece of an answer, a shift in the field. It connects me to yet another question.

The blue shot with gold encircled the lively green world. I felt welcomed & celebrated. I felt the flow inside & out as I walked my path.

Late Winter/Early Spring 2004: The Messenger

$\mathcal{F}$eeling the cool tease, I pulled the warmth from the skies, wandered, gathered, found the opening to my green place, & spread her gifts. I was the messenger.

With a joyful open heart I felt every step, connecting & connected to everything. Stretching, moving, reaching for the magic in the air, the caress of the textures on my eyes. All around me the love, the bliss; I am open.

Reflective, receptive, meeting the moment, carrying the treasures: the trees, the sweet dry air, the white light. All of this is the measure of beauty & of silence.

My hands reach out, the touching is different; illusive yet magnified. There is a direct involvement with my inner workings. The sheath of golden light on textured dripping branches creates a tableau amid the forest backdrop. The vision burns into me. I am breathless. I am suspended in this moment, tears rushing down my face. I feel it from my toes to my scalp. I am pulsating, vibrating, seared by my emotions.

My passage through my green world today was a bit dreamy. With soft footfalls on fluffy clouds, I glide through the labyrinth. I find my way to the inner quiet, my peaceful heart.

Early walk into fairyland, a shimmering veil of light. Cool moistness allows the dense earth fragrance to balance the sweet-spicy-peppery floral tones. Flights of fancy & quiet contemplation continue the theme of balance. Leaving my place, the sun warming my back, I cross the bridge into the amazing new day.

The soothing balm of my path guides my thoughts. I am so blessed, full of joy & wonder. My life is about love, discovery, creativity. The stuff that comes up for me regularly is around judgments, control, detaching from outcome. The people in my life mirror this for me.

I appreciate the subtle gifts from my green world, the shifts in color & scents. I make some placements on nature's altars. I am a small part of all of this & I rejoice.

The delicate rapture of floating through my world, I'm lifted now & again by pieces of fantasy imagery. I feel the terrain under my feet, the nourishment provided by the experience, from my outer to my inner world.

Peace, serenity, connected to my world I am nourished & complete.

The windy night left gray after-affects in my green world. The washed air was full of scent, making my morning meditation a sensual wandering.

The brilliant flood of light paints the trees; a misty glow emanates from the ground, my green world is golden. Along my route I notice a dragonfly grounded, its beauty revealed through its pattern & color & perfect aerodynamics.

Breaking through into the new world, cleansed & gleaming, I'm thrown into a torrent by my own steps, my own thoughts. I steer through dark, familiar underground caverns; finding my way through loving, giving, reflecting, healing. This is how I ground myself, feel myself in my body, connecting to everything, speaking my truth.

Quiet inner journey, I gently allow the outer elements to soothe, to enter, to enhance my reverie. The level of my sleep deprivation has reached the near exhaustion point. My barriers are down.

I walked in patience & receptivity through my glorious green world. She shows me what I need to see & guides my spirit.

The wind made her presence known in my green world today. Her whispers held the coded messages, her turbulence brought infusions of scents to hidden places. Her caress left me in the midst of a memory.

It began as a light & playful walk through my green place. I was thoroughly in my body, enjoying the contrast of the cool mist hitting my bare arms & face & the warm air that was buffering me. Coming out into the openness of the Winter garden, I blossomed into the welcoming trees.

Deep Beauty & Serenity

I deeply felt the beauty & serenity of my green world. I'm walking with a peaceful heart full of light, the array of colors merging with the sounds, textures, scents of this majestic place.

Blissful streaming through my enchanted land today. Golden boughs, berries effusing, red languid shapes forming in the magical forest. Open spaces & dark pathways each beckon to me in their own way. My openness allows me to encompass the depths, the contrasts, the whole.

Peaceful acceptance, receiving the beauty & energy from my green world. Putting things in their place, finding perspective, gifts from my walk. Focus is needed, creating intention….

Glorious early walk into sweet birdsong & busy, rustling squirrels. Long shadows & golden light lead me into cool green, the waning half moon bringing my eyes to the sky. I drink it all in & feel it stretch throughout my entire body, again blessed, again at peace.

Spring spilling over, breathing in that warm dry promise of long drawn out days fading into sparkling dark nights. The stillness in my green world stirs me, finds its way into my recesses. All that is here reflects in the satisfaction of my being.

Opened up as I made my way through my green world, letting my steps guide me. Receiving all the information through my senses, I will process in time…

A walk in nature, the silence of the full reception: blissful, light, contentment spilling over into long sighs.

The light described the sensual lines of the tree. Further on it lit up the maple leaves against the dark trunk of a looming cedar. I walked gently through my green world today feeling & appreciating the light. Amazing morning, heart full to the brim, connected to the life energy of my green place.

As I enter my green place I am full of emotion. Soon I have found the path to my tears & as the first ones hit the ground the wind begins to howl. Then as I look up, a ribbon of blue streaks across my vision & I see in the dark branches a glorious stellar jay. My tears continue as I feel deep excavation at work, radiating from my heart & solar plexus. This has to do with yesterday's wedding: the thoughts & memories stirred by people & events from long ago, a lifetime or two.

Cool tones, warm air, crows & squirrels giving chase. I was moved by the peaceful beauty beckoning me to join in quiet timelessness. I found treasures in moments, found release in memory. My walk today was an exercise in replacing judgments with love. What this did for me was put my mind at ease, filling me with tranquility.

Quiet peaceful appreciation for my blessings, my morning walk & all it brings to me.

Inner journey, cool & gray, walking between black & white.

Quiet walk until deep in the woods I startled a young peregrine falcon. He moved farther into the trees & I watched as he surveilled his territory. Enjoyed the increase of energy as I continued my walk, loving my green world.

Slowly entered, walked my path, quiet appreciation, felt the nourishment, the peace.

Containment & Processing

So much is contained, then processed within me. The joy of my green place lightened my step. New discoveries, flowers, dimensional arrays, quiet feeding. Wind, water sounds, love, gratitude.

Beauty & peaceful refuge, my green world welcomed & encompassed me. I found my quiet voice.

Light tracing details on a single branch
Great blue heron quiet above the small pond,
I am breathing deeply the moist dark earth.

Cool quiet meditation, came upon the young peregrine in the primordial woods. He was on a low branch but as I approached he gradually moved higher & higher. I stood watching him for about a minute, enjoying the mist from the sprinkler.

Solitary patchwork ground, earth textures speaking strongly yet softly; spreading, enlarging into a complete panorama.

I woke to rain in the night. As I stepped out my front door I was bombarded with scent. The rain had revived the sleeping flowers & dried green to elicit layers of separate & subtle fragrance. This was the beginning of my sensual adventure. My green world was experiencing a melodious, lusty bliss. I could feel her receiving the jubilant drenching; her colors deepening like skin during lovemaking. Along the trail the puddles reflected the sky, enlarging the dimension of my experience; rounding, completing; another reference to the cycles, the depths, the layers of conscious & unconscious perception/reality. As I entered the inner woods the alchemy of water & light gave birth to a sensation of shifting worlds, veils moving to invite my participation in this mystical journey.

Happily I find the rain in my walk today. When I am safely inside my green world, the thunder begins. First it sounds like it is being poured out from a box.

Then it seems to be spreading in a circular motion, cracking the air & combining with the sound of the furious pelting raindrops on the forest canopy. I seamlessly move through this dramatic interplay of water music & sky percussion, face to the heavens, drinking it all in.

I was gently encompassed in my green world today; walking, speaking, breathing, spinning, creating a mantra of appreciation, of inclusion.

A nourishing meditation, I moved through emotional intricacies. Stretching through the peaceful bounty, I became a feather carried on the breeze. I hear the whispers of the trees.

Quiet pathway, gentle gifts, my world opens to me.

Sometimes I feel like I'm on the outside, not of this world. I am not caught up in the furious flow, the race to get somewhere. I am somewhere else, caught up in the stillness, looking to reflect, to penetrate & understand.

I walked into my green place, lead by the clouds: feathery fingers of fire. As I emerged from the trees into the open, the clouds had become a fleet of fluffy chariots. Back into the woods in my solitary world, I am contained; there is no sky. The sound of my breathing & footfalls pieces together the rhapsody of my morning.

Golden glimpses throughout my green world; reminders of life's radiance & joy.

A ripe sweet day, opening with golden streams, breezy blue skies, waning faint moon. The path tells me a story & with rapt attention I begin today's journey.

As I enter, connecting with my breathing, I find my tears, my heart, then the thrusting into the mystery. I move through stillness & light, textures of feelings disassembling me, finding pieces of myself strewn about. Returning from the underground river, after bathing in the night, I leave behind a stream of stardust.

A Bit of Stardust in my Head

Into a flurry of green & white, pieces of sky, fleeting energy. I'm walking on the earth not quite connecting. I find my way through, gathering & breathing, still a bit of stardust in my head.

Cool placid place, in color & feel. My thoughts are drifting in & out, part of the flow.

Another entrance into gray white pale blue; trees breathing in the coolness, invigorated. My mind & feet wander, the path is certain, the trees markers for moments of bursting emotion, the fullness of promise.

Got started later, so the sun was higher, changing everything; round, warm, golden profusion. I stopped to study a heron at the pond; I embodied his stillness. I made some decisions that lightened my load: contentment, acceptance, optimism.

I became immersed in the deep sensual beauty of my green world. At times I breathed her, finding no edges, other times sweet tears & release.

Wonderland walk: peace & torment, melting into contentment, ideas emerging.

The morning whispering, I find my holy place amid dappled shade & golden drenched branches. The air tastes of the new day, the perfect beginning.

I walked slowly through my green world today, drinking in the light. I watched the wind in the trees, the reminder of unseen forces, the subtle visibility only of its passing.

Stretching slowly unwinding into my green place, home comfort, the earth pulling me into her womb, her dark recesses.

I felt like I was carrying extra weight this morning; a burden, something unnamed & uninvited. As I tried to purge myself there was that familiar sensation of holding on, of trying to spin straw into gold, to integrate rather than excavate.

I am walking through my life carefully examining that which I will take & that which I must leave behind.

Another waking dream, the walking pushing forward drifts of thought, pieces of semi-conscious detritus & treasure to be sifted & filtered, flavored, consumed again. The passage unhurried, outside the fray: a totality, a lifetime.

I'm in a deep quiet place; the trees are my skin. I feel the earth's rotation as the light translates the essence of me in this moment. When I am here, how can I question the perfection of this life?

Late Summer 2004/An Offering

*W*as welcomed by my green world with daybreak skies above majestic treetops, happy dark fragrant earth, a fallen oak leaf: an open hand holding gleaming droplets of water…an offering.

Walked into the serene pale-skied forest, a subtle shift had occurred. Quiet energy accompanied me as I received the blessing.

A stirring in my green place, the birds were hidden. A story was unfolding, written on the parched falling leaves, the handful of faded blossoms, the moody edge of gray in the clouds. I am inside & outside of this story; mine is one of jubilation & love's celebration.

The wind marked my journey today, sweeping me through the inner recesses, rustling the dry leaves, changing the flow.

I've released something, I feel lighter. I receive the blessings from my green place, the cool moistness invigorating my passage. An exchange has taken place, I feel contentment; I walk in grace.

Marine air was washing over & into me, soft blues & whites caressing my eyes, I entered my green temple. As I moved along the path I asked my father for guidance with my struggles. The next moment I saw two squirrels mating, tails flying. It was just the right lightness & humor to break through my intensity. A gift from my father. I continued my walk, entering one of the chapels in my green place. I stood in reverence surrounded by the gorgeous symphony of birdsong & mystic beauty. I wept, finding compassion for myself through quiet release.

The tender dappled clouds float in pale blue skies. A crow, then another & another glide across the clouds, the sky, drifting past in sharp relief….a cutting through, black obsidian daggers.

Windswept, I found my gifts from the green world, the gatherings: pieces of meaning, ephemeral fragments.

Into the rain I go, inhaling the washed air imbued with the scent of fallen plums. My green world has become the underground river: my unconscious flow, a dark dream. The sharp pain above my left eye brought me to thoughts of my death; brain aneurism….not seriously, just a brief moment. Then I examined how the thoughts reflected in my body: feelings, sensations. I felt at peace, a quiet center of love surrounding me. I then thought about my children, family, friends. I have ended exchanges with all of them in kind loving words. I feel no regrets. I do feel the tug of things undone, unfinished travel, projects, my vision of a cultural center/sanctuary in France. I am grateful & happy to be healthy, strong, soaked to the skin, very much alive.

Late walk, delicate half moon, the gift of stillness, learning patience.

Walking through, watching reflections & passing into feeling, floating, passively observing, miles to go…

My enchanted green world was covered with a glistening web of moisture. I was newly baptized by a bough of cedar as I walked by. Dark stones in moving streams, drops of water making points of light everywhere.

Breathtaking morning, my green world has drunk the ambrosia & transformed. Splendor dripping, lit with golden plumes, she's a palace of plenty.

Stunningly beautiful morning, open & blue, clear & inviting. Entered my church & wrapped myself in her celebration. Found guidance in the stillness of the primeval woods; faith, detachment, deep appreciation, acceptance. Each day is an occasion. Today the last day of Summer!

Autumn 2004/Golden Pavilion

The entrance to my green world was a golden pavilion this morning; nature's opulence fed my senses as I traveled my path. The birds & squirrels were active & noisy, so by the time I reached the inner woods I was ready for the stillness.

The world is wide open; my green place brings me to new realms. Firm steps lead through fragrant peaceful glens, a curtain of textured light, layering green & gold, the perfect sheen: a glorious gift to the eye.

Delicious & tender my green world this morning. I am full to contentment.

Centered in love, freedom, responding to beauty; I am in it, vibrating.

Quiet flow, inner/outer connection; I feel a rush as my heart swells. The clusters of transitional color, a surprise blossom, the sweet rich pungent earth smells all coming together in celebration of this moment.

The light is flat, serving as a neutral backdrop for my forest; the movement & energy contained. Shifts are occurring in the field; new winds, another passing.

Still working on containment, finding more stillness, inner quiet. Chaos is expressed in my environment, work projects, even my social activities.

The veil of mist adds dimension to my green world & to my thoughts. I'm feeling rudderless on a large frothy sea. I pitch from side to side, reaching for my inner ballast. Then as I create equilibrium I realize that I am the sea, the waves, the storm.

A bolder mist enlivens my green world, the tone seeping into my fragmented thoughts & restless spirit. The struggle continues, reflected in everything, everywhere. I feel like a conduit or perhaps a ground wire; part of a larger whole. I know I am receiving that which is outside of me. It reaches my inner tides, directing their flow, their ebb. I am my world, in process…breathing, swallowing, transmuting.

Thoughts of my Father

Thoughts of my father; it's been eight years since he left his body behind & was off to the next adventure. I placed an offering for him in my green place.

The quiet interplay of nature reveals shrouded forms, a peaceful passage. The memories a body carries are poignantly carved into the psyche's musculature. The large mirror is held up to be viewed by the bold, yet to be reckoned with in a distant whisper, under the cover of night.

Morning calm inviting my green world into my release, guidance/teaching. Miles to go, I trust my inner eye & the voice of all my worldly moments compressed into the melody of my heart. I sing my world; I walk into deliverance.

I was walking in a bubble, focusing on the earth, the leaf-littered patchwork carpet. The tears came as I crossed the bridge, a storm of them, frantic & hot. This storm carried me along my path still focused on the immediate feeling of intense sadness. I then experienced brief moments of delight; the burnt sugar smell of the Katsura, the wind made visible stirring the trees, stirring my heart.

Into the rain, I received the cleansing, little by little working towards relief. The forest has a healing effect on me as I feed on her happy moistness. I am beginning my inward travels once again, the dark explorations in search of silent jewels.

*I*nto the heart of the storm's aftermath, I walk through the miles of colorful sheddings. The fabric of nature cushions my feet & takes me back to the sleepless hours listening to the fury. I feel the penetrating sweep, held captive as my racing heart invites the turbulence to enter.

I was filled to the bursting with nature in my enchanted forest. The birds & squirrels came close then scattered when hearing my sotto voce. As my path wound through new colors & textures I could feel myself pass into a realm safe from vacant mechanical living & consuming, the mediocrity of passionless cheap filler junk food thinking. As soon as I found that safety, I plunged back to embrace the totality with & without my judgments, into the place of my heart, into my love.

Tears down my neck, swallowed tears down the back of my throat, grief penetrating & further darkening the unlit passage deep within. I am walking into uncharted regions, blind; just my inside edges translating the messages. Pulsing, searing, resting in carved recesses, glimpses surfacing, but the lion share is waiting to pounce, to roar; another day in another of grief's revelations.

Quiet gentle rinsing from the rain, new shiny waterworld, bubbling stream, adding layers of windblown leaves, staggering color, scent, earthbound transformation living & dying their cycle. Four seasons, separate passages fed by separate lives, choices, loves, dreams. Full circle I ask the wind to take me, claim me, empty me.

The wind has done its work, the path redecorated in hearty swaths of detritus, filling my head with scent & memory.

As I pass through the river of leaves my feet find a musical resistance, a colorful dance. My eye is drawn to the ground & then to the circle of magic light that is this world. As I release myself into its keeping, I feel the magnitude. I float within the confines of my senses reaching the silken sky.

Having discharged avalanches of stored emotion through music, tears & trust, I walk my path with a lighter heart. Through silence I paint serene essences ground from shadows & sighs, the pigments of dreams. These layers of quiet will find voice through the unconscious admixture of souls.

Wonderful wet glistening world, the trees bowing under the water's weight, cradled & caressed me as I walked through. We share the spirit of nature's magnificent bounty. I feel accepted & complete.

I walked through warm still air into a world flooded with scent. The scent became more potent, the evidence of the windstorm littered the ground. She's had a thorough thrashing. The tree limbs, piles of leaves, cones, pods, green branches & berries were everywhere. I was mesmerized by the quiet aftermath. As I neared the end of my path the mists were beginning to shroud the trees. I passed through, recognizing once again the power of the world to reflect my insides; to give me what I need. I am grateful.

I walk on light feet with light heart this morning. I receive a robust welcome from my green world. Clear clean air brushes through blue sky treetops, golden patches warm the leaf river. The reds & yellows shade & shift the landscape, whole sweeps become tunnels of light reflecting the color of fire.

The woods provide deepened tones, rusts & caramel browns. I'm walking through a kaleidoscope as the light peeks in & out of my passage. It is a wild wonderful journey.

I was first beckoned by the sound; the elemental music of the downpour. My path had become a vessel for rivers & lakes, the water dancing & bubbling, reaching out. Forging along I soak in the rain, becoming another stream, moving through, gathering momentum, finding my way.

Wisdom of the Dark Mother

*I*nto the world of rain I walk in celebration. I let it all in, splashing through puddles full of color, leaves layering molting. I brought back offerings for Hecate's altar; she will help me find the wisdom of the dark Mother & peace in the season of death that leads to rebirth.

Swift energetic passage, all the thirsty places in my green world have been quenched.

The world opened up as I walked my path. At the beginning she was quiet, a bit shy, perhaps a little sleepy. As I progressed into her darker places, she let me witness her interior; the scent of mushrooms, fermented leaves, crushed berries. The many birds filled her with their songs & the light was held back until all at once the sky burst into itself with gold, blue, white, the gray edges keeping everything from escaping into infinity.

Cool fragrant morning, the sunlight breaking through to bring my green world to life. As my path opens I follow strands of scent; the early witch hazel, the entrancing Katsura. The autumnal dance has played out; pale stretches of blue setting off the forest in flame. Elegant & brilliant, it moves towards completion & its deep sleep.

There is such a sweet & potent purity to the air & light in my green place. Walking my path is like taking a cool dip in a mountain stream. The experience brings the senses to attention; an abrupt but welcome engagement. Once opened, the whole world enters.

As I near my green world I see the mists moving between two trees, creating a separation, a shadow, a recessed shrouded twin. My walk brings me deep inside myself; the quiet slow rain of leaves releasing, dropping, drifting, twirling, gliding. The slow motion action…is this how we let go when it is our time? Do we dance & spin & float as we descend into death? I think I would like to dance into death. It makes me think of all the death mythology; the symbolism of process, the river Styx, Charon, the drama of life/death/rebirth, Persephone, Demeter, Hades, the bargains, the tricks, the hidden agendas.

I felt peace in the containment of my green world. As my thoughts came, expanded & dissipated, they create the rhythm of place; the heartbeat, the breath, the mantra.

The blue was distant, a promise skirting the gray & white. I left it behind as I entered the woods; world of texture & color, the full surround. Then just as I think I cannot hold another sensory fragment, I'm filled to bursting with a cascade of scent & sound. As I cross the bridge, leaving my woods, the wind sweeps through the trees, shaking loose a migration of yellow butterflies taking flight then slowly drifting to earth.

As I crossed the bridge into my green world I felt the cold penetrate my jeans. The frost blanketed the open fields flashing white in the bright sun. I feasted on the newly burnished surroundings, the accents & contrasts; a receptive journey.

I found a new openness, the light unobstructed, new shapes & surprises. My world is breathtakingly beautiful; around each corner a treasure to behold. A gold-washed tableau sparks memory, warmth, the fire within. Another stretch of colorscape evokes a dream state, again the inward journey.

Frost abounding, there is a hard crust on the earth. The cold brings tears to my eyes creating a mist between my world & me.

The air was incredibly sweet, an invitation to open up to the big wet world. I ventured through, enjoying the artistry of the leaves, the glow created by the carpeted tunnel. About midway the rain texture started changing, slivers of white shot to earth. I closed my eyes & felt crystals of wet snow land on my eyelashes & nose. By the time I got home it was again rain.

Brilliant morning with frost covered rooftops drenched in pink-gold-apricot light. In my green world the open spaces have been dusted with sparkle, the silver white articulating each blade of grass, each leaf. The ground has become solid, rigid, shooting the cold into my feet. My world has become aloof in her beauty, with a haughty elegance. She continues to intrigue me as I follow my path.

I enter fairyland on the momentum of my excitement. The child in me walks through winding passages, seeing magical pathways, gleaming landscapes. The morning bursts forth with possibilities.

There was an icy sheen on my world this morning, the sky a Nordic blue. My green place is a stern mistress, keeping me at arm's length. But I felt a boldness & conquered the frozen pathway, finally reaching the gate to my inner passage.

Much of my walking meditation I spent looking at the ground, the designs & patterns of fallen leaves, the spongy frozen texture of the earth. Later my world & I opened up to each other; a flood of warm light & sensation. Flash frozen world: I walked through it in a dreamstate, part of an enchantment. I saw people & placements as symbols & messages. I returned home in a golden light, with a peaceful heart.

I found my world soft & fragrant, a whisper of mist hovering just above the earth. The rain had pierced her hardened veneer & she was warm & open to me. Above the treetops the blue washed sky held a few puffs of rosy clouds lit from below. I feel just on the edge of a revelation, like someone is trying to tell me something but I can't quite hear or understand. I will pay attention to all the details, the signs. Perhaps it is a puzzle or a test.

Quiet receptive energy, I followed the path of tiny scattered maple leaves; fallen stars leading me to some far off destination. In the sheltered inner woods some trees have held onto their leaves, their color just beginning to change. They have a different clock. I breathed in nourishment from my green world, bringing it to my deep center, but I still feel a bit like a fallen star.

I walked into the peaceful morning; the sky was faraway blue, the color from which dreams are spun. The moon rode high on a long drifting cloud & my feet were barely touching the ground.

Glorious pristine morning, I breathe in the sweet icy air as I move through my green place. The trees take their turn in the spotlight- a brilliant red leafed witch hazel has receded into the background now that her branches are bare. A neighboring vine maple steps up with bold yellow & bronzed reds & greens. It is the visual music of life, of process, the beauty of the precipitous edge. Expression equals meaning equals identity.

I experience renewed contentment through release as I stay the course, moving through. While I'm pulling in the stillness within my primeval chapel, I notice a shimmering, a portal; my green place enchants me.

I'm having a dreamy walk through dripping, musical woods; standing apart in my warm coverings, the wind & rain taking liberties with my green world. The transforming leaves emit a new light; a higher frequency, as the concentrated peak energy is expressed before the decline. So much of that energy is present, it feels as though other dimensions are in residence.

I was fully embraced by my wondrous wet & jubilant green world. I marveled at the coursing streams & waterfalls, puddles growing into small ponds, the glossy sheen on brilliant leaves, layered, scattered reds & yellows & bronzed greens, rusts, oranges, browns. I became a creature of this wild place; drinking in the powerful transitional beauty, absorbing & relishing it entirely.

New forms, new skin, my green world has been deluged. Scattered, torn, blanketed, flooded, uprooted, she continues to express her transcendent beauty. I feel complicit as I walk through the storm of her transformation, as if I were an integral part.

Emotional journey, I make my way through subterranean depths, not much surfacing. I find my patience & plod step by step, feeling the richness, appreciating each moment.

My walk today allowed my active mind to find a safe haven, an integration. I am both energized & soothed by my green world. In expressing love & gratitude I'm able to receive a deep peacefulness of spirit.

I felt a deep connection moving through, a sense of timelessness, then the taste of winter to come: a reckoning.

Sweet Explosion of Grief

Sweet explosion of grief, the mix of sadness & reverence for life, life's energy, essence. A death, an ending, bringing one to revisit, to interpret, to integrate, a thoughtful process, an uncovering. Take away the armor, the protection; there is a fire-hot entrance wound, an opening to the gory fleshy bloody truth. We are of blood & bone, we pulse with the song of the universe, we dance our rhythms within its voice, its exacting presence containing us while we exhibit our selves, each cell revealing, crying out: I am, I live, I have meaning, I die.

Welcomed by an otherworldly light, I ventured onto my path. There was an ease, a fluidity to my walk; my subtle world enveloped me in peaceful thought.

White light breaking into mist: a walk of twists & turns, a pair of ducks on a pond...paradox?

Breathing in, receiving, listening, translucent awareness.

I was filled to bursting by my green world, but as the rhythm of my sobs became the rhythm of place, I expanded to receive even more. I took in every morsel; the plant decay with its dark rich energy, the startling beauty of the yellow-leafed Linden, the quiet texture of windblown empty trees. It was a journey through pain into thanksgiving, of introspection & merging, a discovery of self-love through immersion & acceptance.

Inward journey beyond words.

I walked blindly, led by my inner darkness. The rain formed a circular sound bouncing off the fallen leaves. As I descended onto the banks of my underground river, I yearned for the light (& lightness). The weight of my sadness slowed my pace, dimmed my perception; it has found comfort lodged in my silent depths.

I felt closed off & dark entering my green world. She had patience with me &

reflected my stark mood. As I released & released through cavalcades of tears, she held me & eased my pain.

Sunlight opened my green world, streaming through, making visible vapors crawling up the strong cedars. Further along, dark leaves hung from tall Magnolia branches as unlit lanterns in a faraway dream. In the open spaces the dogs appeared, playful & spirited. I wanted to run with them; their energy stayed with me as I smiled all the way home.

A quiet palette, an empty canvas, digging deep to find the first brushstroke. I put my brush down; it is time to receive the gift of passage.

Shades of gray, dappled mist, the sounds of industrious squirrels mixed into long stretches of pastoral landscape. Crows accenting bare branches while filling the sky with their cries.

With an open blue sky, I'm drifting through peaceful rivers, earthy scapes, the ever-changing green world. My thoughts are traveling inward, gathering dark obscure references as blankets for eventual slumber.

Early entry into subtle textures, the wind opening a gate; a shift into new sight, new possibilities. A hummingbird, its soft tapping voice, a form of Morse Code, suspended high, hovering, then in a streak of flight, gone.

Quiet rhythm, syncopated to my footfalls, gently caressing the living earth; fragrant, rich, ever changing.

As I stood in my primeval chapel I watched my vaporous breath combine with the breath & energy of the trees near me. Then when I reentered the open space I saw the sky on one side pouring its frothy storm-lit covering over the clear blue morning.

Frosty gleam stretching along the open rolling grasses, monochrome sky closing in, wrapping around the shrinking green place. Quiet pulse, the dreams of ancient, sleeping trees.

I seem to be looking for the way in; a gate, a door, a glimmer of light. Until I find it, I'll be on the outer road, feeling the tug, the twinge of almost-recognition.

I entered my green world closed up, in pain, disconnected. As I walked, thoughts came to me. I was flooded with a sense of disillusionment. I felt a total fraud, my life a meaningless, empty shell. The trees were silent, the streams meandered, my tears came. Everything remained outside, beyond my reach. More tears, the heaviness shifting slightly, the clenched wet heat, the heaving thrust, a stilted rhythm. I am gasping for air, life's breath/blood/meaning. I'm fighting to escape this tiny blurry swollen-eyed hell.

Water sounds everywhere; I travel light of foot through swirls of mist & rain. The light changes as I move through, the leaves lining the earth, softening the edges. My heart is peaceful; I receive the blessing.

The Cast of Familiars

Solitary, I'm warmed by the goodwill of my green place, the cast of familiars. I find my heart/my home in the wandering, gathering, opening.

Effortless walk, I took in all the miniscule elements marking my course. The berries in clustered array sprinkled color throughout otherwise barren scapes. The wind & the early light created playful havoc with the trees.

Caught up in my thoughts, I drifted dreamily through my green place. About halfway I emerged through color & form, opening to the beauty & excitement of the morning.

A gust of wind greeted me as I left my house. The stark damp world surrounded me. As I made my way through my green place, the infrequent gifts of color marked my passage. A pair of hummingbirds swooped in & out of view. The squirrels seemed more contemplative, a brief suspension of their usually focused tasks. The crow sounds shattered the globe of gray monotony, awaking nature's soporific cover.

Beautiful morning greeting from soft cloud pillows nestled in almost robin's egg blue skies. Inside my green world a crow was giving chase to a hawk; but the line became blurred in the cat & mouse game. Pungent scents, dreamy bird sounds, echoes amid naked branches.

Wide open sky, blues fading to white, subtle shifts spinning. I am alone in my green world, humbled by its power, its magnificence, its terrible beautiful perfect truth.

My walk was a healing, my breathing a ritual, my tears marking the beginning, the opening. The expression of fullness, piercing joy edged with sadness. Underneath the pulse the breath the mantra I am I am I am.

Going deep, falling into it, becoming it. My walk today was a different kind of gathering; a pulling into myself, gently finding the pleasure of my inner voice. My path a winding garland strewn with delicate blossoms & glistening boughs, light-filled droplets & many-colored berries. Living in the darkness, cherishing the light, drinking in the potent message.

Something has shifted within me. I am able to receive transcendent joy directly to my heart, the immediacy of the beauty, the blast to my senses, the totality of experience.

Soft gray backdrop, serene pathway opening to fluid thoughts, I look for the balance of lightness & richness of connection; senses sparked, fed, quiet inspiration.

Began my journey with a moody sky; high contrast, sunlight, billows of raindrops. Within my green place there was a shift into subtlety. In the deep woods I stood with unfocused eyes & watched the world breathe; the movement of leaves being hit by drops of water, the mist from my exhalations, the life current running along a smooth branch, the shimmering; an invitation through a portal.

Christmas 2005

Christmas morning quiet, I find I am bursting with love for my children, bursting with memories of Christmas mornings past, stockings, the tree, sparkle, laughter, wonder. The emotional memory of holiday is complex, multi-dimensional; part fantasy, longing, anticipation. As I pass through my green world I receive the gift of scent, from the pale apricot azalea & the Chinese honeysuckle.

I felt nourished by my forest; thoughts sifting away, the breath becoming a meditation, the walking an alignment with the earth.

Sunlight, sculptured clouds, crows decorating the skeleton trees. The blue sky patches teasing my senses as I walk on quenched earth, the air washed clean. In my green world, porcelain blossoms painted by fairies, a single spray of open flowers on the winter cherry. Along the stream the dead brown-leafed plants become a group of monks marching in a solemn row. The Mahonia explodes skyward, its yellow flowers from Peter Max's brush, its scent a magnet for a clan of tiny hummingbirds. In my deep woods chapel my angel-eagle treetop waves at me from afar & gifts me with the tears I'd been holding at bay. I find my way home feeling whole & full with nature's bounty.

Through the delicate cold white edge, the hardened skin, I move further into my green world. Air pockets are revealed beneath frozen abstract art in nearby puddles. Within deep quiet I come upon a pair of fancy birds, their intricate fine feathers a pleasurable sight as they perch on the vacant bones of a tree. I am in a place of contemplation, feeding on sweet morsels such as this, keeping close to home.

White crested hills, sled tracks, dogs chasing kids downhill on boards (that sounds like the dogs were on boards but it was actually the kids). Partway into my walk on white pathways & dark sheltered trails, the snow started falling again, flakes the size of silver dollars. Coming around the corner near the gazebo the light wasn't as flat & I tried to see as far as I could into & through the falling snow. It was amazing; very trippy, a feeling of endless perspective, a stretching of sense reality.

In a lovely calm my green world is open to me. I sift through memories, connecting with melodies, letting everything flow through me. I feel blissed.

Walked under multicolored enchanting sky, thoughts whirling about my head, never quite able to leave them behind. Crossing slippery paths, patches of sheen, icy patterns, I stopped to admire the water pine leaning windblown over the stream.

As I begin my walk I am aware of the cold biting into my legs, the wind hitting the exposed skin of my face. I find catharsis midway & weep within the safety of my woods.

It's very cold, clear & bright; there are spirals of ice filling puddles & unforgiving earth beneath my feet. Inside my green world I am insolated & isolated. The evergreen rhodys are contracting, leaves curling into funnels, any remaining blossoms have taken on a darker hue, a crystalized concentration of color. My walk is contained, quiet, serene. I'm feeling a bit like one of those blossoms.

In the welcome light I feel golden as I walk, with arctic clarity, through puddles filled with beach glass, a long shadow cast. I carry music, rhythm, tone along my passage, thoughts subverted into melody.

Into the majestic white world I am the child. I am here to play, to run, spin around, fall, get up. Through quiet windings marking my path, I am light, at peace.

Amid juicy noisy water sounds, I sloshed through melting snow, skidding, sliding. My green world was closed in, still heavy with snow. I walked my path full of story, full of melody.

Crow sounds, moody sky, into the world I go. The mists have settled in the open spaces & later I find them in hidden places. I take them in through my eyes & my lungs. Just as I reach the winter garden, surrounded by fragrant witch hazel, the rain begins & pulls the perfume onto me; I am drenched, cleansed & celebrated.

I entered the forest of quiet, a moving witness to chubby squirrels & fine feathered crows. As I reached the primordial chapel it drew me into its stillness & as I found myself enmeshed within, I realized there was a curtain of mist protecting my ceremony.

As I venture into the cold brilliant breathtakingly beautiful world, I feel the weight of my thoughts. I spread them out within the sacred woods. I feel the pieces of my mind & body return to me in a new form.

Seeking refuge I found solace in a holy place, surrounded by nature. My thoughts are scattered amid the plants & trees, dissolved into the mists. My weariness & strain have dropped to the earth like a heavy coat. As I marked my passage with reverence & gratitude, love flooded into my heart.

She opened to me, she showed me under her petticoats, the invitation to a new way of seeing, an acute ability, an extended sense. Drenched, cleansed, I am able to mix new colors for my painting. I am able to combine the glossy sheen of the clay within the soil, the color of emptiness-apathy, with the vibrant hue of purposeful blossoms, budding with all their might, opening before my very eyes.

What is important to me? What comes through to me in any given situation? The essence of beauty, finding my heart engaged, the wholeness of cycles, the faith within, following to completion, letting go of outcome.

I'm quiet inside. I am contained inside my world within a world. I walk & feel & flow & pull into myself. There is a delicate breath, a silent sigh.

This day is new, I'm breaking new ground, seeing with new eyes. Laced with sadness, my walk is splendid, breathtaking & inward. Each step gives me the faith that only moving forward can give.

I live in the richness of my inner & outer world.

I feel an inner calm, the pieces of my walk find logic in the flow. I feel like I'm experiencing several levels of consciousness at once.

Embraced by my green world, I feel safe & full of wonder. Many feelings run through me. I feel like a vehicle, a sponge, a conduit. I am slowly letting go, examining my heart, my intention. I am slowly shedding my skin.

I walked in love with my green world, encompassed in her safety, magnitude & flow. The moving is a reverence, celebration, a reentry into myself.

Misty quiet, I experience a long meditation in my primordial chapel. I feel a shift within as the drops fall onto leaves creating movement & light; I receive this directly to my depths.

Into the Night

Into the night I strode, blue sky with carved dark clouds showed the beginning of first light. My green place was empty & solemn, gradually opening to me.

Blue darkness, morning emerging clear. My gentle world holds me close, allows me to pass through with humble steps & gasping sobs. The grief is deep; I am shifting, vulnerable to what is next.

Faith in process, inviting in the world, I now have several more toggles on my control panel. Love of animals, primordial chapel, sacred sequoia grove. They are states of emotion-trance, their center is love; my center is love. I am working on my questions & how to surrender to my imagination.

A single gull appears in the mottled blue-white sky. I am a terrestrial being feasting on sensual delights. I gather scents & colors, smooth textures, glowing moss-covered shapes. I speak the language of the trees, the water, the cool air. My prayer goes deep inside me & then radiates outward.

Gathering & expressing energy & experience, I feel like a magnet. My walking meditation today is full of activity & information.

My green world was a receptacle for my flow, my thoughts, words, stories, discoveries. The rain created the background, the sounds & rhythms.

My green place transports me; I am taken to another place & time, inside a dream. I pay admission to enter; my sadness split open, examined, excised, but not entirely. Such weight I carry right now; I can't see all that I'm packing. Perhaps I will find a way to set myself free.

I am fragile as I walk my path, as my green world swallows me. I have surrendered to a new exploration; one in which I have no visual context. It is a foreign place, but I invite it within. As it enters me I feel fluid & in vibratory form. It is strange

& exciting. My mind is struggling to understand, to place it in my known reality. I must let go of that reality & embrace the uncertainty.

Into my open heart the green place fills me; I am learning to let go, to be the flow. Sadness, grief, relief, curiosity, stillness, exploration inside & out, my path continues to surprise & feed me.

Again my green world is a healing. After receiving stillness I become the water; I am not separate.

Mist, rain, torrents of tears, my insides revealed; finding resolve through giving up the struggle. I turn inside out, upside down, stretch into a new world, imagining myself, filling myself up.

Feeling whimsy, I enjoy my walking meditation. The air & light speak of spring & there are subtle signs from the trees & plants. My world reminds me that my center is love & my life is full.

Breathing in my green world, being cleansed & brushed & blessed, I am just passing through, a shift in the light, a rustle of footfalls. The joyous water song, the mud slap, the perfect pink flowers, the scents flooding in. This is the world of all possibilities.

I feel the earth below my feet, barely having to touch, the action light & easy. I love my green world. I find peace here; I find myself.

Merging with the mist I birth new pain, new intensity. I feel safe to unleash my fury & sadness.

I am a child within all of this; my heart is full of love.

The fog gently enfolds my green world. I am still on a long road looking into the distance. I pull in what is around me; I breathe the essence, the color & form.

Quiet wet gray, I felt my green world from her underside, her still but potent inner places. From the outside I gathered Mayan ruins in my primordial chapel & rippled pond song, as I neared the fragrant open spaces.

I step into my enchanted green world. She offers the perfect refuge for my spirit. I wander searching for places where I can express what I feel, what I imagine, who I am. In my sanctuary here I spread within & throughout, expanding to touch the light.

I stood in front of the altar & engaged my green place. She swept into me with all her wind & light & beauty & intensity. I felt her entirety, breathing & weeping & stepping in.

I worked through some sadness, some barriers, feeling much rumbling within. It finds me sometimes unaware. I am so full of emotion & life: all the mix. I will keep writing, to tap the flow, to pulse & express in words, colors, flashes of textured thoughts. My ideas are flying, taking off into space, twirling, spiraling like in my primordial chapel this morning.

My walk revealed parts of myself to me. Passing through, I saw reflected back, the form of my life; I felt everything make sense.

Stirring the thoughts of the past few days, bringing them the perspective of today, I quietly let in my green place. I am making room for new lessons & transformations. My faith continues to bring me new worlds.

More letting go, walking by, loving myself, seeing the beautiful golden girl full of light. I'm learning, moving through, letting things change around me, not having to grab onto anything, just allowing everything to be.

Began my walk in sadness. I could not contain my tears. Cries burst from my throat. I tried to move the emotion from my heart, but it wouldn't budge. The sense of isolation weighed me down. I've only lightened my load a little. I need to open to my own love, my own heart.

The light is returning, an infusion bringing life to the colors & surface. I'm feeling lighter & less held down by the sadness in my heart.

Beautiful morning, lots to think about, lots to wander through, weeping, letting go, being open to learning, uncovering. I'm searching for my light & lightness; the beauty & wonder is reaching me, continued excavation is necessary.

A new beginning, stretching beyond, the promise of a day all its own. My time alone, the cherished steps, the flowers, roses, the emerging spring.

Coming out of the house I was greeted by the sweet rain smell, the washed earth, washed sky. As I found my way through my green place, I came into the canopied glen & there was a rhododendron in bloom. The blossoms sat astride large elongated leaves like perfect little cakes: pink with white icing.

Persephone Will Soon Be Set Free

I entered my green world in a closed unhappy state with shallow breaths & gray thoughts. I gathered pieces of sparkle, color & fragrance along the way; I'm starting to open from the inside. There's a struggle taking place within me, perhaps Persephone will soon be set free.

Early walk, quiet spirit, I'm gathering, appreciating, letting it be.

A walk in prayer with soft focus: a journey, just learning to be.

Peaceful opening of my heart; beauty evoking sadness, full force & deep. Prayer, alignment with Our Lady, Goddess Madonna, light pouring into me.

Lovely quiet walk, feeling centered; gathered many visual & tactile delights, fragrance hits. I'm working on finding balance & flow, being open to new worlds.

Finding my focus, I follow my path through my golden, sparkly green world. I release some sadness & some intense appreciation for the beauty & magnificence of this place. There seems to be a connection between the two emotions.

Walked in prayer with Quan Yin, Our Lady Guadalupe & St. Francis. I asked for the eyes of a child to learn to be open & accepting of a new world. Later in my walk I imagined/saw/felt myself lying on my back on the top of a gigantic flower, gazing up into a sky of multi-colored luminous shimmerings (blue peace-symbol acid circa 1969). The flower was slowly revolving & I felt warm & safe. St. Francis, Quan Yin & Our Lady were with me.

I'm finding my way; every day a new path, the same path. Breaking through, attention, focus, comfort through prayer.

A dark wet passage, I felt closely contained inside my hooded coat. Midway I broke free; the rush of cool damp air on my face like a sweet breath after being under water.

Spirited yet relaxing walk, I found my rhythm & my thoughts were mostly grounded. There are always tasks & new vistas to find. I am capable & willing.

Found lots of twists & turns, bumps & rocky spots on my path today. I want to speak my inner truth, to find the delicate senses with which to feel my world. I want to strengthen & refine this vessel to further express & transform through love & imagination.

I asked to be opened, to receive new worlds, new senses. My primordial chapel provided vistas beyond normal scope; the Temple of Inscriptions has found its place there; the spirals have returned. The flowers have continued to seduce me with their lushness, translucency & color.

Into the singing rain, textured sounds woven into the whites & grays. I found a pair of mystic trees standing within the mist; they enchanted me. In my chapel I became an instrument for all that surrounded me; tones, colors, textures, raindrops; I swayed & vibrated, taking it all in.

Elegant spring morning, golden light, new blossoms, washed air, pale to deep blue sky. My green world opened me up yet again; she grounds me, but also allows me to fly.

Light beaming into me, my green world held me, comforted me, enlightened me. She's opening up in her spring finery, sweeps of abundant color, vibrant textures, sweet & pungent scents. My blessings are many.

My prayers were to the Chimayo Madonna. The outside world was blustery gray & wet. I walked with openness & blessings, gathering fragments for an offering.

Pieces of thoughts drifting by, I bring my green place's beauty into me; I feast on the fresh new buds, the lively tender spring essence.

New openings, revelation, my green place leads me into myself. Today it felt like a beginning.

Woven greens & golds, pinks, whites, soft tapestry lit from within. Patience, trust, quiet, asking for clarity.

Plunging into sorrow, the pool of tears, finding my reflections; a shift, a change, feeling a loss.

Into the wind, a delight to come upon carpets of fleshy petals, the large magnolia blossoms decorating as they drift about. The cherry trees are in full regalia. The sky revealed new colors in the changing light.

Blue carved into gold, windblown pink petals are forming pathways of delight. I'm thinking, dreaming, meditating, passing through.

A bit of frost, clear brilliant skies piercing through pinks & whites, overflowing cherry blossoms.

There seemed to be a dog theme today on my walk. I enjoyed the playful interaction, the lightness; so much new life & beauty everywhere.

Divine birdsong flooded through the celebrating blossoms; the light & scented air perfecting the experience.

A breeze carried me through my green place. I bore witness to the workings of a new Season. I am grateful to be part of the mystery.

Sweet scents were my companions on my walking meditation. The rain had washed thousands of petals off the cherries & magnolias; decorating the pathway & the evergreens. I was surrounded by beauty.

I was inside the rain that inhabited my green world; the sounds & wetness penetrated throughout. The blast of sensation was further increased by the profusion of color & scent.

Enchanted forest, petals leading the imagination through doorways of light & color. Pools connecting underground tunnels, caverns intercepting golden fields, warm scented blossoms, other worlds, kaleidoscopes, playful opening to my inner self.

Quiet inner journey, trust in my prayer, my place in the world, allowing what comes in to find where it fits. Letting go of frustration & judgment, getting closer to surrender, not having to figure it out, understand. I invite my world to enter my heart, my breath, to guide, love & fill me.

Majestic sunlit experience, dog-filled, Bronx Mojo, morning magic. I added more juice to my primordial chapel button. I also installed a time-release mechanism for the tubes of light that Mark gave me. Perhaps he'll come along on my journey. As I left, the tops of my shoulders & arms tingled & itched slightly, as if I were releasing something or peeling away a layer.

As I examine the world through my particular lens in this moment, there lie the deep colors & fragments of decay & design. I search outside my senses, a glimpse, a recognition, a piece of timeless memory. It bends & flows as I make my way through, traveling with golden light, love in my heart.

Cool clean wonderment, fresh winds, petals flying, defining, observing, softening. I released & felt support from my green world. I am so grateful & feel complete.

Lightly stepping through my green world, a beam changing focus, expanding, finding wonder in the new life of spring's expression. I'm breathing, feeding, contemplating.

Within my primordial chapel I feel woven in, implicate. I see the pattern of life energy in the islands of moss, tree limbs pulsing, spirals, fallen blossoms, fire-streaked leaves. My prayers bring me closer, a folding in, a lightness. As I walk I connect with my symbols; those pieces of visual-emotional consciousness which keep me from spinning out into space, into the void. I feel an implicate lightness connecting to my very being.

Teaser/Epilogue

I continued my daily walking meditation after moving to the French countryside. After a couple of years I discovered that I was known locally as "La Dame qui marche" (the woman who walks). For me this felt like a gifted Native American name & I was honored to carry it.

In my second book, this old soul, this Woman who walks, will continue on her path, her moving meditation through life, sharing her wisdom, stories & vision. This Quantum Tale for children of all ages will bridge two cultures, two languages & untold universes. I hope you will join her.

Printed in the United States
By Bookmasters